ROVERS

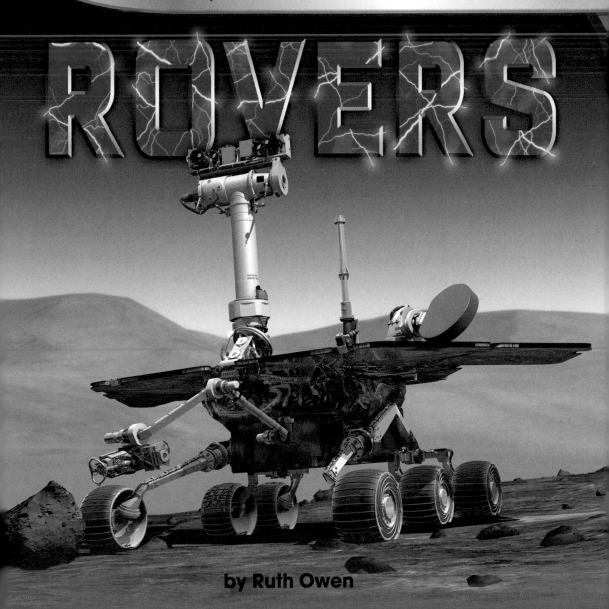

by Ruth Owen

PowerKiDS
press™

New York

Published in 2015 by **The Rosen Publishing Group, Inc.**
29 East 21st Street, New York, NY 10010

Library of Congress Cataloging-in-Publication Data
Owen, Ruth.
Rovers / by Ruth Owen.
p. cm. — (Objects in space)
Includes index.
ISBN 978-1-4777-5851-9 (pbk.)
ISBN 978-1-4777-5855-7 (6-pack)
ISBN 978-1-4777-5853-3 (library binding)
1. Roving vehicles (Astronautics) — Juvenile literature. I. Owen, Ruth, 1967-.
II. Title.
TL475.O94 2015
629.43—d23

Produced for Rosen by Ruby Tuesday Books Ltd
Editor for Ruby Tuesday Books Ltd: Mark J. Sachner
US Editor: Sara Antill
Designer: Emma Randall
Consultant: Kevin Yates, Fellow of the Royal Astronomical Society

Photo Credits:
Cover, 1, 5, 9, 11, 13, 15, 16–17, 19, 21, 23, 24–25, 27, 29 © NASA;
7 © Science Photo Library.

Manufactured in the United States of America
CPSIA Compliance Information: Batch # CW15PK: For Further Information contact
Rosen Publishing, New York, New York at 1-800-237-9932

CONTENTS

ROBOT ROVERS

In the past 50 years, hundreds of different spacecraft, space probes, satellites, and other objects have blasted off from Earth.

Some of these objects, like the *Voyager* probes, have traveled billions of miles (km) across our **solar system**. Others, such as the Hubble Space Telescope, are orbiting Earth just a few hundred miles (km) above our planet's surface. A few have actually landed on the Moon and Mars. Their missions have been to study our space neighbors up close. These are the rovers.

A rover is a wheeled vehicle designed to explore the surface of a moon or planet. Most rovers are robots. They are remotely controlled and can do the work of humans in dangerous places.

On the surface of Mars, the average temperature is -85°F (-65°C) and the air is made up of poisonous gases. A robot rover can be designed to withstand this hostile environment. It is able to study Mars, while its human controllers remain safe on Earth, millions of miles (km) away.

SPACE OBJECTS FACT FILE

Like all robots, a rover has a computer "brain." Scientists and engineers design and upload instructions into the rover's computer brain. The rover then acts on those commands.

Curiosity's human team on Earth celebrates on August 6, 2012, as the rover safely lands on Mars.

An illustration of the rover *Curiosity* that is exploring the surface of Mars.

THE FIRST ROVERS

On November 17, 1970, the *Lunokhod 1* rover landed on the Moon. It was the first-ever rover to land on another space body, such as a moon or a planet.

Lunokhod 1 was built and launched by scientists and **engineers** from the **Soviet Union**. It flew to the Moon in a spacecraft named *Luna 17*. The rover had eight wheels and looked a little like a bathtub with a lid. During the day, **solar panels** in the lid captured the Sun's energy to power the rover's batteries. At night, the rover closed its lid and went into sleep mode.

Lunokhod 1 analyzed soil on the Moon and sent more than 20,000 images of the Moon's surface back to Earth. The rover's mission lasted for 11 months until it finally lost contact with Earth in September 1971.

On January 15, 1973, *Lunokhod 2* landed on the Moon. It explored the Moon's surface for about four months, and sent more than 80,000 images back to Earth. Both rovers are still on the Moon's surface.

SPACE OBJECTS FACT FILE

The name *Lunokhod* means "moon walker" in Russian. *Lunokhod 1* traveled about 6.5 miles (10.5 km) over the Moon's surface during its mission. *Lunokhod 2* covered an impressive 24 miles (39 km).

Earth

Solar panels

This illustration shows how *Lunokhod 1* may have looked on the surface of the Moon.

THE MOON BUGGY

In the late 1960s and early 1970s, NASA sent astronauts to the Moon as part of the Apollo space program. On Apollo missions 15, 16, and 17, a rover went, too.

The Apollo astronauts landed on the Moon in a spacecraft called the Lunar Module (LM). During the first three Moon landings (Apollo missions 11, 12, and 14), the astronauts left the LM and explored on foot. Walking on the Moon was not easy, because the astronauts had to wear bulky, protective spacesuits. On the later missions, however, they used a rover. This allowed them to travel farther from their landing craft and visit more places to collect samples from the Moon's surface.

The four-wheeled lunar rover, or Lunar Roving Vehicle, was the size of a car. In order to transport it to the Moon inside the LM, the rover could be folded in half. NASA built four lunar rovers. Three went to the Moon, and the fourth was used for spare parts.

SPACE OBJECTS FACT FILE

The lunar rover was nicknamed the "moon buggy" because it looked a lot like a dune buggy that people use for driving on sand dunes and beaches.

This photo shows NASA scientists testing out how the lunar rover will be folded up for storage inside the Lunar Module.

Apollo astronauts Charles M. Duke Jr. (in the left-hand seat) and John W. Young training in a lunar rover on Earth.

DRIVING ON THE MOON

Each lunar rover was designed to carry two astronauts and their equipment.

The rover was fitted with a TV camera that could be remotely controlled by NASA scientists back on Earth. This allowed the mission control team to watch the astronauts as they explored. Coverage of their excursions could also be beamed back to Earth to be shown on TV.

A rover was powered by batteries that gave it enough power to travel about 57 miles (92 km) during a mission. The astronauts never traveled farther than 5 miles (8 km) from the Lunar Module, however. This was in case the rover malfunctioned and the astronauts had to return to their spacecraft on foot.

At the end of each Apollo mission, the astronauts took off from the Moon in the top half of the Lunar Module. The bottom half, where the rover traveled, remained behind and was not needed for the return journey. So the rovers had to stay behind, too. They are still on the Moon today.

SPACE OBJECTS FACT FILE

A lunar rover had a top speed of 8 miles per hour (13 km/h). In total, the three lunar rovers traveled just over 56 miles (90 km) between them during the three Apollo missions.

Apollo 16 astronaut John W. Young works at the lunar rover alongside the Lunar Module.

Astronaut Eugene A. Cernan in the Apollo 17 lunar rover on the surface of the Moon.

THE FIRST ROVER ON MARS

Having successfully landed rovers and even people on the Moon, the next challenge for space scientists was to deliver a rover to another planet.

The goal of the Mars Pathfinder mission was to send a small spacecraft, or lander, and a rover to Mars. On July 4, 1997, that goal was achieved. After a seven-month journey across space, the lander touched down on the surface of Mars—but not before bouncing a few times! Thankfully, its airbag cushioned the landing. Then the tiny rover, named *Sojourner*, trundled from the lander, becoming the first rover to visit another planet.

Moving at about 2 feet (0.6 m) per minute, *Sojourner* explored hundreds of square feet (m) of the planet's surface. It analyzed soil and rock samples to discover what chemicals they contained. *Sojourner* was originally expected to keep working for just seven days. But it kept on going until September 27—a truly unexpected 84 days!

SPACE OBJECTS FACT FILE

The name *Sojourner* means "traveler." The rover was named after Sojourner Truth, a 19th century American **abolitionist.**

This photo shows NASA scientists preparing *Sojourner* for its mission. The rover was 2 feet (61 cm) long, 1.5 feet (46 cm) wide, and 1 foot (30 cm) tall.

Here, *Sojourner* is surrounded by the lander's airbag on the surface of Mars. The rover is flattened for traveling.

The lander transmitted more than 16,500 images of Mars back to Earth, including some that show *Sojourner* at work.

THE TWIN ROVERS

Nearly six years after *Sojourner*'s successful time on Mars ended, two more rovers left Earth on a mission to study Mars.

Carried aboard a Delta II rocket, *Spirit* blasted off from Cape Canaveral, Florida, on June 10, 2003. Its partner, *Opportunity*, was launched in the same way on July 7, 2003. Each Mars Exploration Rover was packed inside a spacecraft aboard its rocket. After detaching from their rockets above Earth, the spacecraft began their 300-million-mile (480 million km) journeys across space. Just over six months later, on January 3, 2004 and January 24, 2004, the rovers reached their destination.

On reaching Mars, a lander inside each spacecraft separated from the main craft and began its descent. At this moment in its journey, the lander had to slow its speed from 12,000 miles per hour (19,300 km/h) to zero in just six minutes!

At 30,000 feet (9,000 m) above the planet's surface, the lander deployed a parachute. Close to the surface, the parachute detached. Then, protected by a covering of airbags, the lander bounced hard on the rocky surface of Mars. The lander then unfolded, like the closed petals of a flower, to allow the rover to emerge and begin its mission.

Spirit blasts off at the start of its mission aboard a Delta II rocket.

An artist's impression of a lander floating onto the surface of Mars protected by airbags.

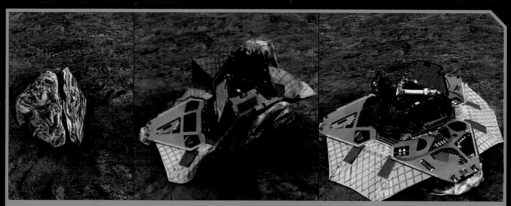

The airbags deflate and the lander unfolds to reveal the rover inside.

SPACE OBJECTS FACT FILE

Small pieces of metal from the fallen World Trade Center buildings were used in the construction of each Mars rover.

ROBOT GEOLOGISTS

The Mars rovers' primary mission was to study Mars's rocks and soil. The rovers were searching for ancient clues that would tell scientists back on Earth if Mars had once been a warmer, wetter planet.

Human geologists explore rocky terrain on foot, investigating the rocks they find with handheld tools. *Spirit* and *Opportunity*, the robot geologists, carried out their work in a similar way. Controlled by human operators back on Earth, the rovers were designed to drive up to 130 feet (40 m) every day. As they moved over the surface of Mars, the rovers studied rocks and soil samples.

SPACE OBJECTS FACT FILE

Each Mars Exploration Rover is just under 5 feet (1.5 m) tall, 5.2 feet (1.6 m) long, and 7.5 feet (2.3 m) wide. It weighs 400 pounds (180 kg).

Each rover was fitted with a robotic arm that contained cameras. The cameras were designed to zoom in on a rock and take highly detailed photos. Back on Earth, human scientists could analyze the photos as if they were looking at the actual rocks through a magnifying glass.

This illustration shows one of the twin rovers at work on the surface of Mars.

The camera aboard *Opportunity* took this photo at the edge of the Erebus crater.

A SUCCESSFUL MISSION

During their investigations, *Spirit* and *Opportunity* made a very important discovery. They found evidence that there was once liquid water on Mars.

Today, there are no rivers, lakes, or oceans on Mars. There is only frozen water at the planet's north and south poles and frozen water underground. So was Mars once a water-covered, warm planet like Earth? Why did the planet's **climate** change? And when did this change happen? Studying how and why Mars changed may help scientists answer questions about Earth's history and its future.

In May 2009, *Spirit*'s wheels became stuck in soft soil. Scientists on Earth tried to recreate the problem on Earth using a test rover. They hoped they could devise a plan to free *Spirit*. Unfortunately, nothing could be done. In May 2011, *Spirit*'s mission was terminated.

As of September 2014, however, *Opportunity* is still exploring Mars and going strong. A mission that was due to last just 90 days has continued for more than 10 years!

SPACE OBJECTS FACT FILE

The twin Mars Exploration Rovers have been so successful that two asteroids have been named *Spirit* and *Opportunity* in their honor.

This photo taken by *Opportunity* in September 2014 shows the rover's own tracks on the surface of Mars.

Solar panels

This image of *Opportunity* (seen from above) was created from a series of selfies taken in spring 2014 by the camera on the rover's long arm.

CURIOSITY GOES TO MARS

With so much still to discover, NASA sent another rover, named *Curiosity*, on a mission to Mars in 2011.

The SUV-sized rover was packed inside a spacecraft. The spacecraft was then launched aboard a rocket on November 26. Once outside Earth's **atmosphere**, the spacecraft separated from the rocket and began its 354–million–mile (570 million km) journey to Mars.

After eight months in space, the spacecraft reached Mars traveling at around 13,000 miles per hour (21,000 km/h). As it traveled through the planet's atmosphere, the spacecraft slowed down. Then the craft's parachute opened, further slowing the craft to around 180 miles per hour (290 km/h).

As the spacecraft approached the ground, the descent stage craft emerged and lowered *Curiosity* to the ground on tethers. *Curiosity* touched down in an area named Gale Crater on August 6, 2012.

SPACE OBJECTS FACT FILE

Unlike previous rovers, *Curiosity* was too large and heavy to bounce onto the planet's surface surrounded by an airbag. Using the descent stage craft and tethers to lower the heavy rover to the ground was a huge design and engineering achievement.

Curiosity blasts off from Earth aboard a rocket.

The heat shield, or bottom, falls off the spacecraft to reveal *Curiosity* and the descent stage craft.

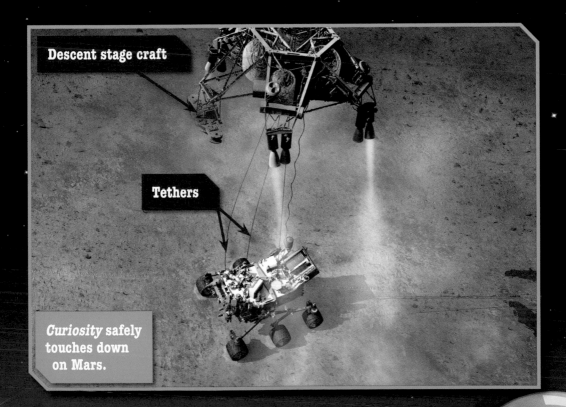

Descent stage craft

Tethers

Curiosity safely touches down on Mars.

CURIOSITY'S MISSION

Curiosity's mission is to look for clues that Mars was once a suitable place for life to exist.

If there was life on Mars, it would not have been intelligent alien beings, but **microscopic** life forms called **microbes**. The first living things on Earth were microscopic microbes. Could Mars have once been home to microbes, too?

Curiosity is a mobile **laboratory**. It searches for rocks that formed in water. It also analyzes soil and rocks to find out if they contain chemicals that could be a clue to the existence of living things. The rover has a drill to break up rocks for samples. It also scoops up samples of soil from the ground. *Curiosity* also uses a laser to vaporize thin layers of rock. Then it analyzes the vapor to identify the chemicals in the sample.

Along with its scientific investigations, *Curiosity* sends weather reports back to Earth. It also uses its 17 cameras to take photos and make movies of Mars.

SPACE OBJECTS FACT FILE

Curiosity is 10 feet (3 m) long, 9 feet (2.7 m) wide, and 7 feet (2 m) tall. Its arm is about 7 feet (2 m) long. The rover can travel at 100 feet (30 m) per hour.

Curiosity took this photo of its first contact with a rock on Mars. An instrument called an Alpha Particle X-Ray Spectrometer is investigating the rock to discover what chemicals it contains.

This illustration shows *Curiosity* using its laser to heat up rock.

DRIVING A ROVER

It might seem that driving, or controlling, *Curiosity* would be just like playing a computer game, but it's a very complicated process.

The closest Mars and Earth ever get is about 35 million miles (56 million km) apart. Usually, the distance is much farther. This results in a signal delay of up to 20 minutes between Earth and Mars. Therefore, it's not possible to tell *Curiosity* to go left or right and get an instant response because the commands take a long time to reach the rover.

This photo shows *Curiosity*'s twin on Earth. This twin rover can be used to test out tasks before *Curiosity* is asked to do them.

A copy of one of the Mars Exploration Rovers

A copy of tiny *Sojourner*

In order to safely control *Curiosity*, every second of the rover's day is planned in detail. When the Sun sets on Mars each night, *Curiosity* takes a break. Its human controllers on Earth work through the Martian night planning every action that the rover will take. They also plot every inch (cm) that *Curiosity* will travel. When morning comes, the instructions are uploaded to *Curiosity*. The controllers then tell *Curiosity* to start work and the rover follows the carefully planned commands.

Curiosity's twin

SPACE OBJECTS FACT FILE

Curiosity is able to think for itself. It uses its cameras to keep watch for hazards. This keeps it from toppling over a cliff or crashing into a large rock.

A ROVER SUPERSTAR

Curiosity has made several important discoveries and, as of late 2014, is still hard at work on Mars.

Just seven weeks after landing on Mars, Curiosity discovered a dried-up streambed. This confirmed that billions of years ago, there were flowing streams on Mars. Curiosity found traces of sulfur, nitrogen, hydrogen, oxygen, phosphorus, and carbon when it drilled into a rock named "John Klein." Finding these chemical ingredients shows that some areas of Mars had environments that were friendly to life.

Curiosity has also studied levels of **radiation** on Mars. In the future, human astronauts may visit Mars. Radiation can be very harmful to the human body, so Curiosity's results will help scientists plan future missions and keep astronauts safe.

Not all of Curiosity's space "firsts" have been scientific. On August 6, 2013, Curiosity celebrated one year on Mars by becoming the first device to play music on another planet. The piece of music it played was Happy Birthday!

SPACE OBJECTS FACT FILE

Social media makes it easy for everyone on Earth to keep in touch with Curiosity. The rover regularly tweets and posts messages on Facebook.

A hole drilled in the John Klein rock by *Curiosity*.

Curiosity sends selfies back to Earth. This image was pieced together from shots taken at different angles, so it was possible to leave out the arm holding the camera.

Curiosity's stunt double, named *Scarecrow*, tests maneuvers on Earth. Then detailed instructions can be uploaded to *Curiosity*.

INTO THE FUTURE

Sojourner, *Spirit*, *Opportunity*, and *Curiosity* have provided scientists with huge amounts of information about Mars. The exploration of Mars will go on, however.

NASA is currently planning to send another rover to Mars in the year 2020. The Mars 2020 rover will be similar in size and design to *Curiosity*.

The rover's mission will be to study how Mars's rocky crust formed. The rover will look for clues to help us understand what the climate of Mars was once like. It will also be the first rover to actively look for signs in rocks to see if microbes once lived on Mars.

What discoveries will the Mars 2020 rover make? Maybe it will find signs of past microscopic life on the planet. Perhaps it will find something incredible that we've not yet imagined. We do know one thing for sure. As the rover carries out its work and beams its findings back to Earth, millions of people around the world will be waiting to hear what the rover has to tell us.

SPACE OBJECTS FACT FILE

In preparation for future human missions to Mars, the Mars 2020 rover will test if it is possible to extract oxygen from the poisonous air on Mars.

It takes a team of hundreds of people to design, build, and land a rover on Mars. Here, a team of scientists is shown building and testing *Curiosity*.

A scientist tests *Curiosity*'s camera.

Curiosity's mission control room.

GLOSSARY

abolitionist
(A-boh-lih-shuh-nist)
Someone who calls for
an end to a particular
practice, especially
slavery.

atmosphere
(AT-muh-sfeer) The layer
of gases surrounding a
planet, moon, or star.

climate
(KLY-mut) The average
temperature and weather
conditions in a particular
place over a long period
of time.

engineers
(en-jih-NEERS) People
who use math, science,
and technology to design
and build machines such
as cars and spacecraft.
Some engineers design
and build structures
such as skyscrapers and
bridges.

laboratory
(LA-bruh-tor-ee) A room,
building, and sometimes
a vehicle, where there
is equipment that can
be used to carry out
experiments and other
scientific studies.

microbes
(MY-krohbz) Tiny living
things, such as bacteria,
which can only be seen
with a microscope.

microscopic
(my-kreh-SKAH-pik)
Only visible through a
microscope, not with the
naked eye.

NASA
(NAS-ah) The National
Aeronautics and Space
Administration, an
organization in the United
States that studies space
and builds spacecraft.

probes

(PROHBZ) Spacecraft that study planets, moons, and regions in space. Probes do not have any people aboard, and are remotely controlled by scientists on Earth.

radiation

(ray-dee-AY-shun) Energy that is radiated in waves, such as light from the Sun, or in particles, such as radiation from uranium.

satellites

(SA-tih-lytz) Objects that orbit a planet. A satellite may be naturally occurring, such as a moon, or an artificial satellite used for transmitting television or cell phone signals.

solar panels

(SOH-ler PA-nulz) Panels made up of a number of solar cells that capture the Sun's energy and use it to make power, such as electricity.

solar system

(SOH-ler SIS-tem) The Sun and everything that orbits around it, including planets (and their moons), asteroids, meteoroids, and comets.

Soviet Union

(SOH-vee-et YOON-yun) A former nation made up of a group of republics in parts of Europe and Asia. The Soviet Union broke up in 1991, creating a group of independent nations, including Russia, Ukraine, Kazakhstan, and Georgia.

WEBSITES

Due to the changing nature of Internet links, PowerKids Press has developed an online list of websites related to the subject of this book. This site is updated regularly. Please use this link to access the list:
www.powerkidslinks.com/ois/rover

READ MORE

Forest, Chistopher. *Robots in Space*. Mankato, MN: Capstone Press, 2012.

Hamilton, S.L. *Robots & Rovers*. Edina, MN: ABDO Publishing, 2011.

Rusch, Elizabeth. *The Mighty Mars Rovers: The Incredible Adventures of Spirit and Opportunity*. New York: Houghton Mifflin, 2012.

INDEX